ALEX AND FRIENDS

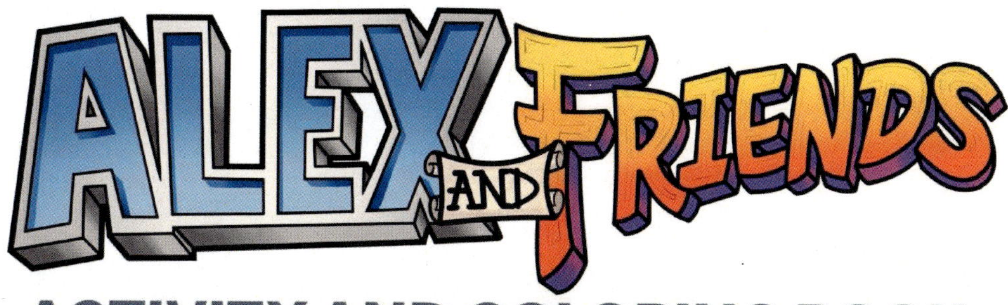

ACTIVITY AND COLORING BOOK

By: Robert Liddell

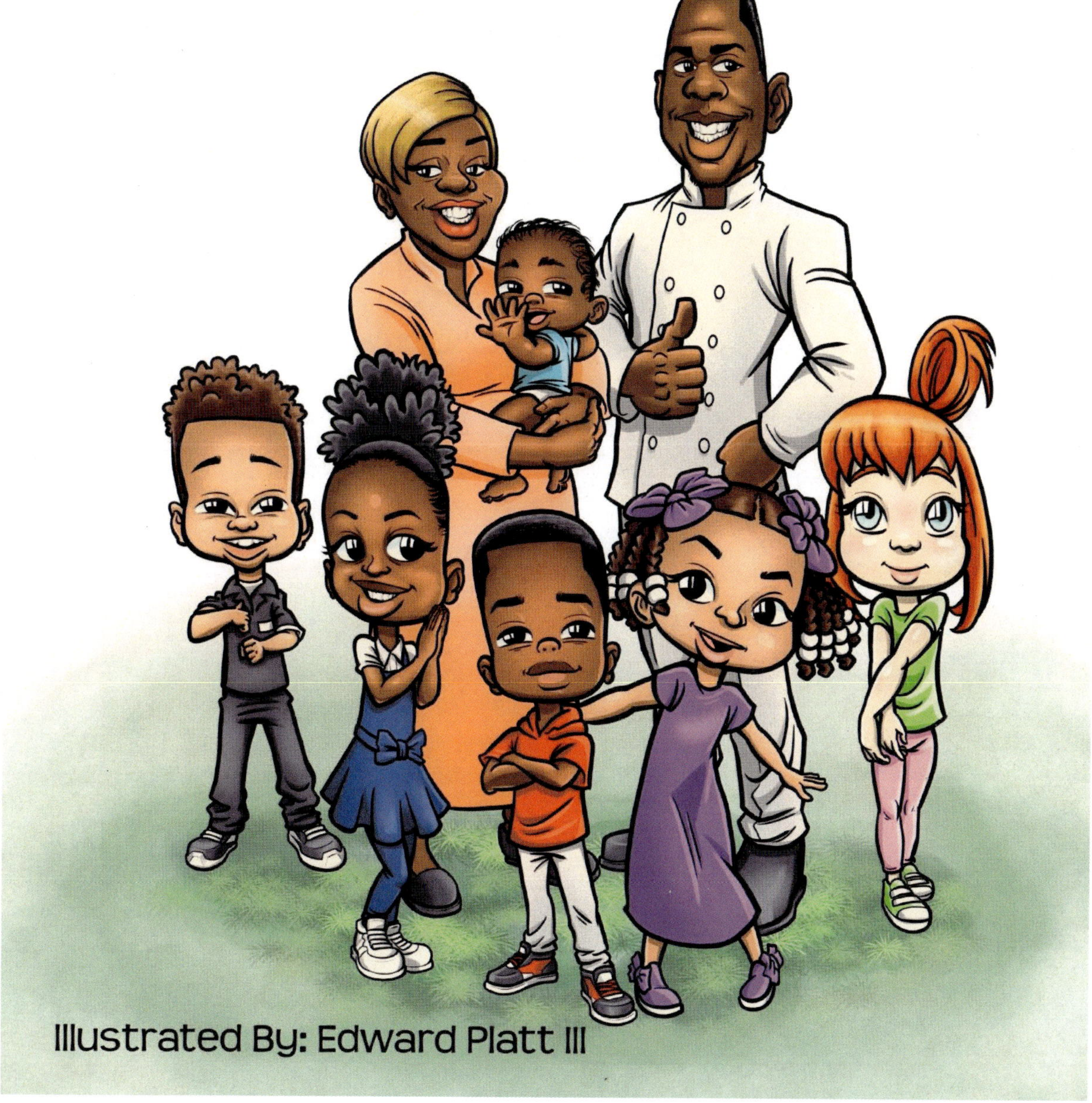

Illustrated By: Edward Platt III

Chef Rob's
Ten Commandments
For Success
1. Pray
2. Eat Healthy
3. Honor Thy Mother
4. Honor Thy Father
5. Dress Appropriate
6. Keep Good Hygeine
7. Aways Study
8. Exercise
9. Ask Questions
10. Never Give Up

TRACE THE LETTERS

A B C D E

F G H I J

K L M N O

P Q R S T

U V W X Y Z

WORD SEARCH

Toni loves cheese pizza. Help her find a few words to describe a great pizza.

M	C	Y	J	X	O	L	I	V	E	S	O	P	D
N	C	V	X	G	R	A	C	I	A	S	B	L	U
S	U	H	D	C	R	K	Y	Q	U	Y	Z	V	V
P	B	A	I	E	U	Q	A	V	B	W	E	T	R
I	I	Y	U	C	N	I	B	O	E	P	S	E	D
N	F	G	H	J	K	A	K	X	L	M	L	T	Z
A	L	P	M	C	Q	E	D	E	L	P	Y	L	E
C	H	E	E	S	E	I	N	A	P	T	B	Y	A
H	N	Y	M	Q	U	X	Y	A	E	H	A	C	B
M	T	P	M	K	D	J	E	Y	P	O	C	Z	S
B	Z	O	W	P	Y	N	N	I	P	R	O	U	A
Y	S	A	O	N	I	O	N	S	E	S	N	G	B
V	R	C	A	P	T	A	A	A	R	M	U	Q	R
O	E	Q	S	A	A	S	A	U	S	A	G	E	O
R	V	T	M	U	S	H	R	O	O	M	S	A	S
G	Q	O	U	X	L	P	A	L	D	W	M	I	O
Y	T	A	P	E	P	P	E	R	O	N	I	G	U

1. Spinach
2. Chicken
3. Pepperoni
4. Pineapple
5. Bacon
6. Onions
7. Mushrooms
8. Olives
9. Cheese
10. Tomato
11. Bell Peppers
12. Sausage
13. Gracias
14. De nada
15. Sabroso

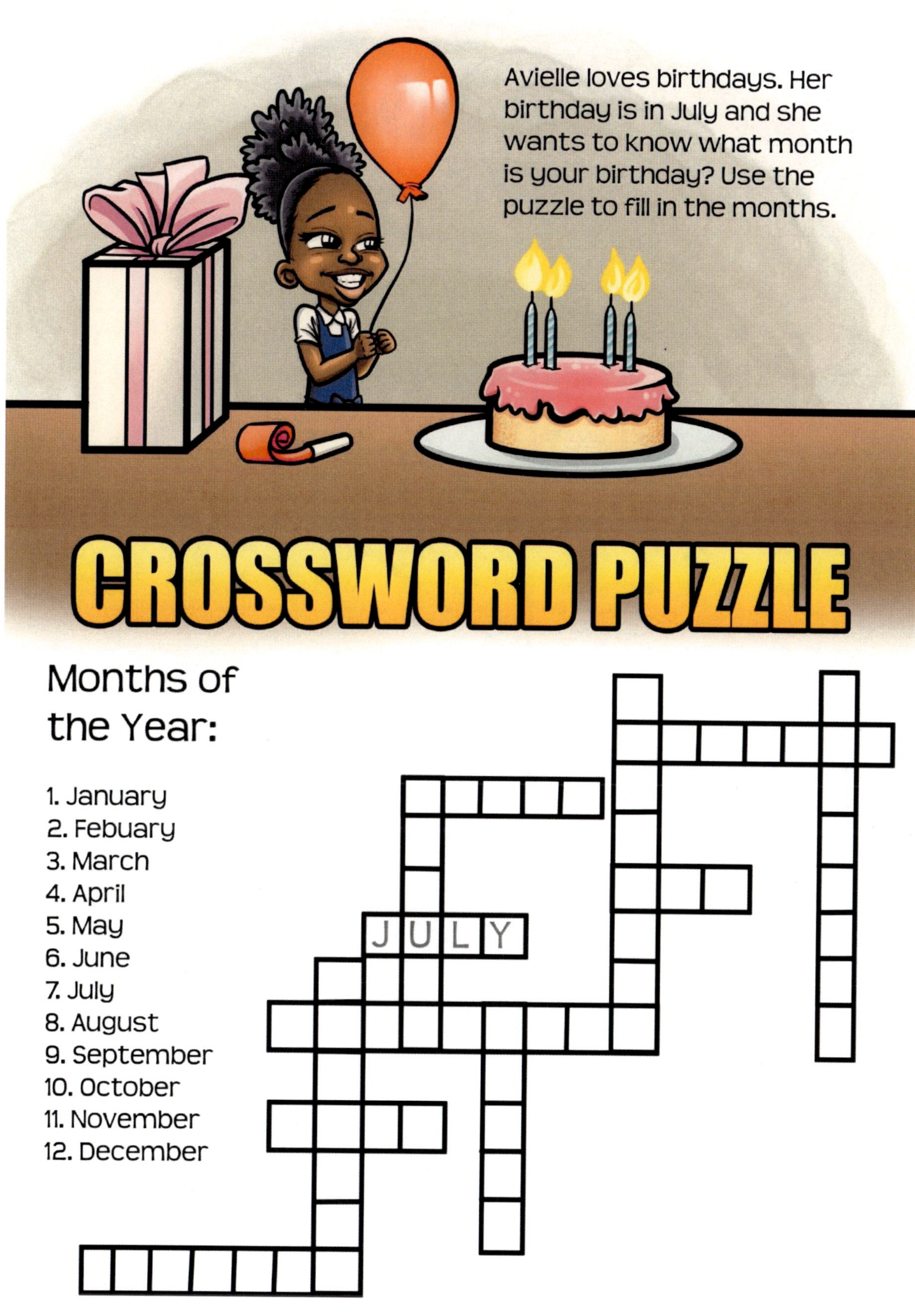

Months of the Year:

1. January
2. Febuary
3. March
4. April
5. May
6. June
7. July
8. August
9. September
10. October
11. November
12. December

Fill in each area of the wheel with the right color.

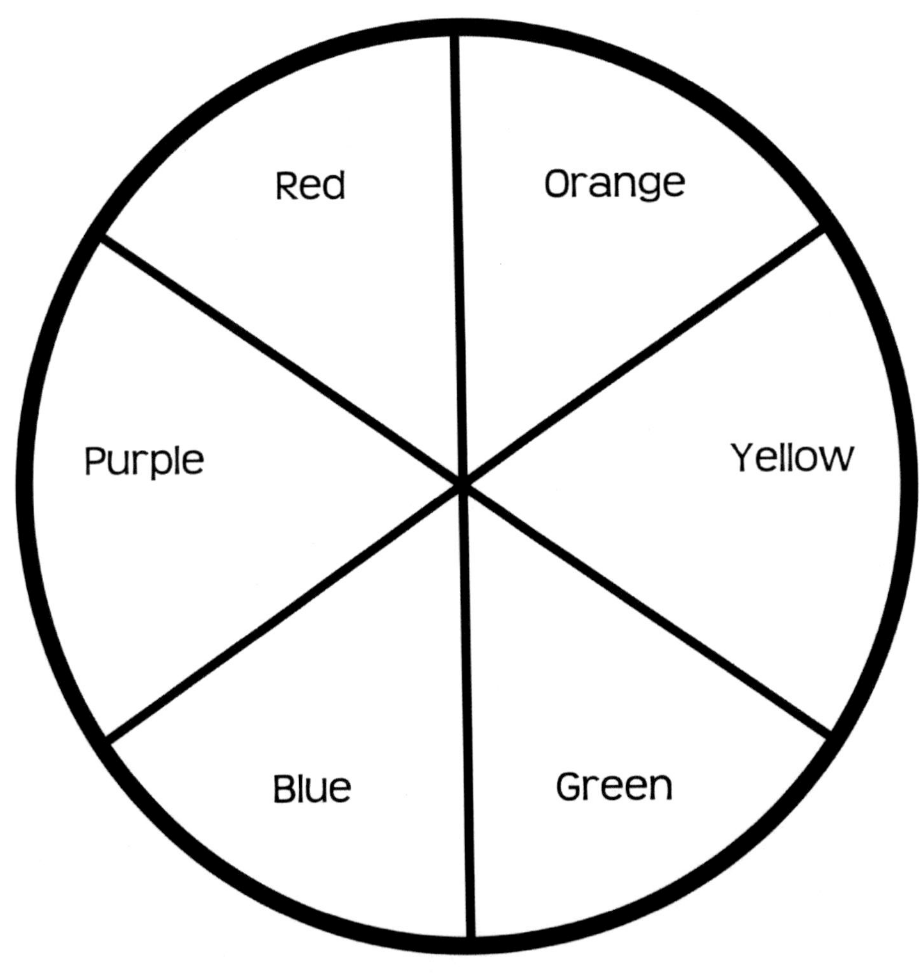

MATCH THE SHAPES

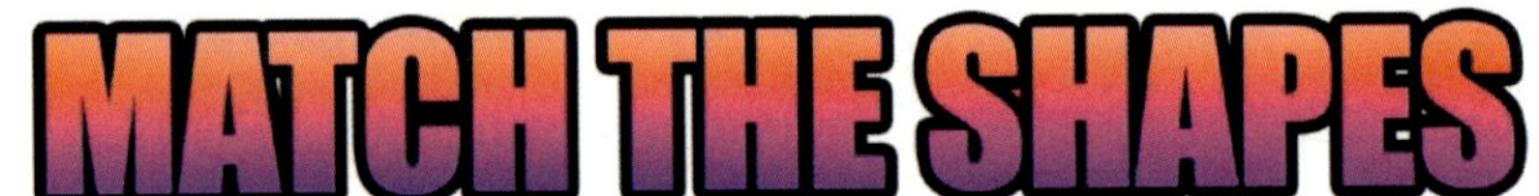

Help Mekhi match the shapes by drawing a line to the correct shape.

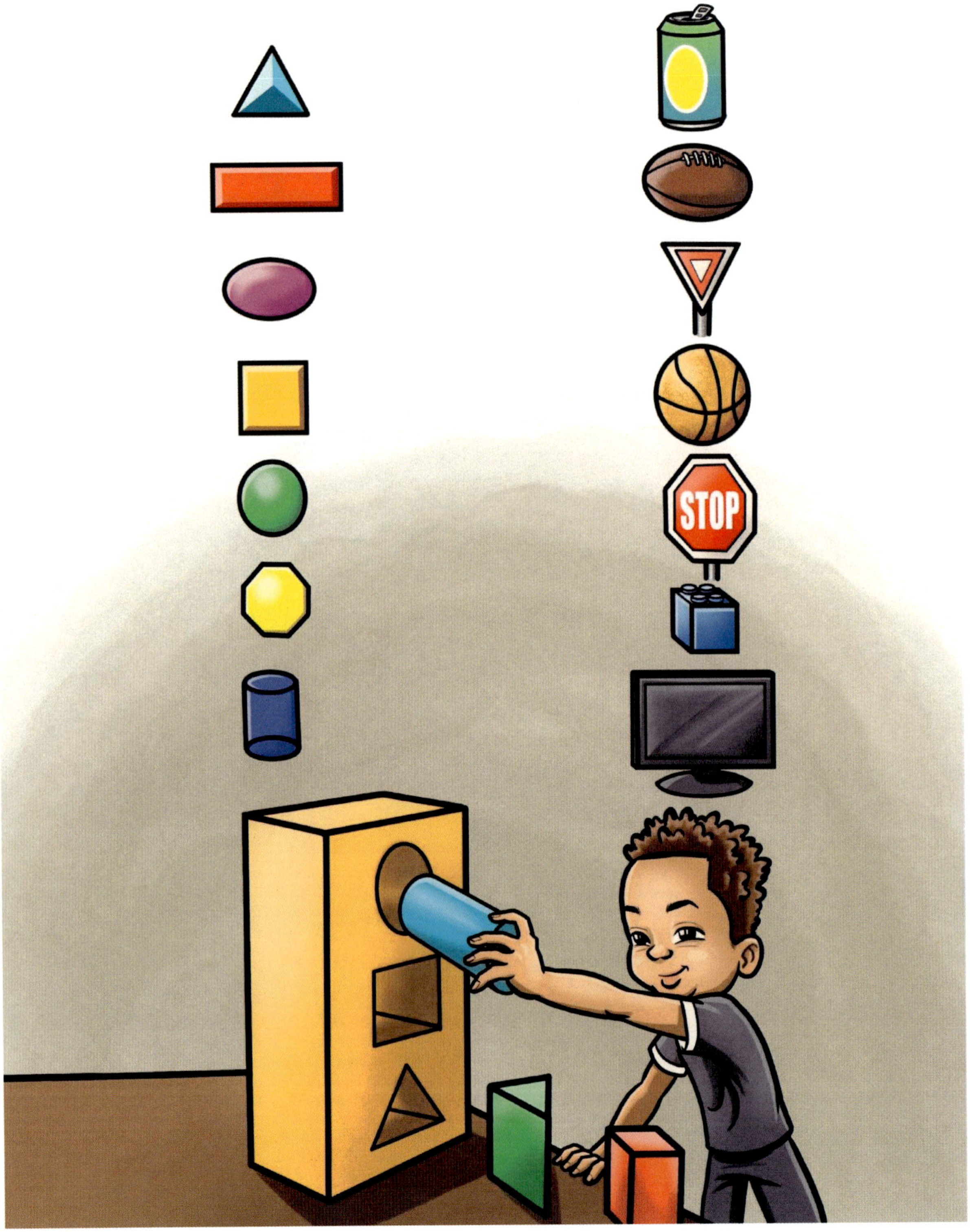

DAYS OF THE WEEK

Fill in the correct days in the chart for yesterday and tomorrow according to the days already filled in.

Yesterday	Today	Tomorrow
	Monday	
	Tuesday	
	Wednesday	
	Thursday	
	Friday	
	Saturday	
	Sunday	

STUDENT OF THE MONTH
Jae'vyon wants you to draw a picture of yourself!

CONNECT THE DOTS

Emily loves to eat healthy snacks.

Connect the dots to draw the tools Emily will use to enjoy her snack.

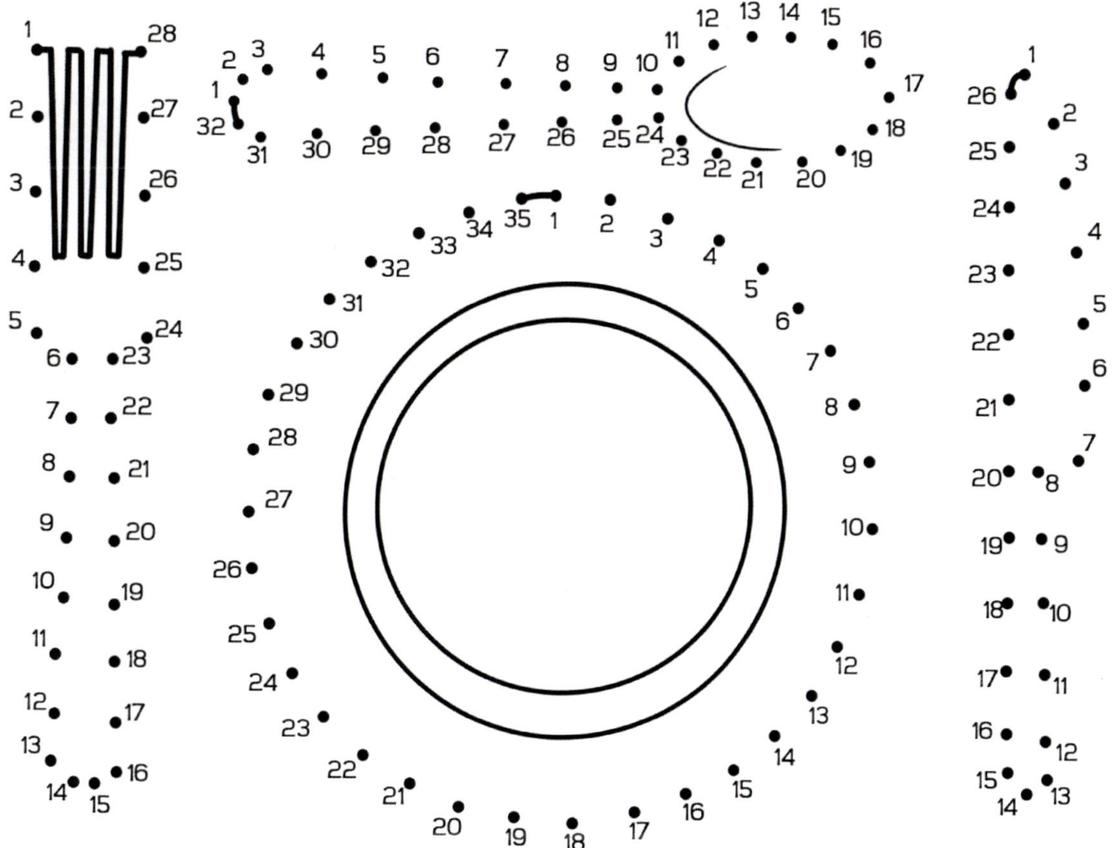

Hundred Chart

Tracing

1	2	3	4	5	6	7	8	9	10
11	12	13	14	15	16	17	18	19	20
21	22	23	24	25	26	27	28	29	30
31	32	33	34	35	36	37	38	39	40
41	42	43	44	45	46	47	48	49	50
51	52	53	54	55	56	57	58	59	60
61	62	63	64	65	66	67	68	69	70
71	72	73	74	75	76	77	78	79	80
81	82	83	84	85	86	87	88	89	90
91	92	93	94	95	96	97	98	99	100

Baby Alex helps his grandmother and father prepare a dinner for the family. Would you like to help?

Follow the instructions on the next page.

LET'S EAT!

COOKING WITH LOVE

This recipe yields 2-6 servings.

Savory Chicken Gravy

Butter 1/4 cup **Unbleached All-Purpose Flour** 1/3 cup **Chicken Broth** 2 cups **Salt & Pepper** 2 tablespoons	Melt butter in a saucepan on medium high heat. Add the flour until it becomes a paste and slightly turns brown. Slowly incorporate the chicken broth with a whisk. Whisk constantly until it thickens. Once thickened, add the chicken drippings and serve hot.

Burnt Orange Carrot Puree

Carrots
3 pounds peeled, cut into 1/2-inch rounds
Sugar
4 tablespoons
Fresh Orange Juice
1/3 cup
Butter
1/2 cup (1 stick), cut into pieces, room temperature
Fresh Ginger
1 1/2 tablespoons minced
Orange Peel
1 tablespoon grated
Fresh Lemon Juice
1 tablespoon
Honey
1 tablespon

Cook carrots and 3 tablespoons sugar in large pot of boiling salted water until carrots are very tender, about 25 minutes. Drain well. Return carrots to same pot; stir over medium heat until any excess moisture evaporates.

Meanwhile, bring orange juice to simmer in heavy, small saucepan over medium heat. Add butter, ginger and orange peel,whisk until butter melts. Whisk in lemon juice and remaining 1 tablespoon sugar and honey. Purée half of carrots and half of juice mixture in processor until smooth. Transfer to large bowl. Repeat with remaining carrots and juice mixture. Season to taste with salt and pepper. (Can be prepared 1 day ahead.) Cover and refrigerate.

Herb Roasted Roma Tomatoes

Extra Virgin Olive Oil
1/4 cup
Fresh Thyme Leaves
1 tablespoon
Garlic Cloves
2, finely minced
Kosher Salt
1/4 teaspoon
Roma Tomatoes
10, cut in half lengthwise

Preheat oven to 350 degrees. In a medium bowl, stir together olive oil, thyme, garlic, salt and black pepper. Toss tomatoes in mixture until coated. Place tomato halves cut side up on baking sheet. Spoon remaining oil mixture over tomatoes.

Transfer baking sheet to oven and cook for 30 minutes depending on size of tomatoes. Remove from oven and cool completely.

Roasted Asparagus

Asparagus Spears
2 bunches thin and trimmed
Olive Oil
1/4 cup and 1 teaspoon
Garlic
1-1/2 cloves minced (optional)
Kosher Salt
1-1/2 teaspoons
Black Pepper
3/4 teaspoon ground
Lemon Juice
1 tablespoon and 1-1/2 teaspoons (optional)

Preheat an oven to 350 degrees F. Place the asparagus into a mixing bowl, and drizzle with the olive oil. Toss to coat the spears, then sprinkle with garlic, kosher salt, and black pepper. Arrange the asparagus onto a baking sheet in a single layer.

Bake in the preheated oven until just tender, 12 to 15 minutes depending on thickness. Sprinkle with lemon juice just before serving. To remove woody ends, grab stalk of asparagus at either end and bend until it snaps or cut with knife. It will naturally snap where it starts to get tough.

Creamy Red Mashed Potatoes

Medium Red Potatoes
8, quartered,
Garlic Cloves
3 peeled
Butter
2 tablespoons
Heavy Cream
1/2 cup, warmed
Salt
1/2 teaspoon
Parmesan Cheese
1/4 cup Grated

Place potatoes and garlic in a large saucepan. Cover with water. Bring to a boil. Reduce heat; cover and simmer for 15-20 minutes or until potatoes are very tender. Drain well and add the butter, milk and salt, mash. Stir in cheese.

Pan Seared Chicken Breasts

Chicken Breasts
4, boneless, skin-on
Smoked Paprika
1 tablespoon
Kosher Salt, Onion Powder, and Ground Black Pepper
Light Olive Oil
1-2 tablespoons
shallot
1, minced
Garlic Clove
1, minced
Chicken Stock or Chicken Broth
1 cup
Fresh Thyme
2 sprigs
Fresh Rosemary
1 sprig
Unsalted Butter
1 tablespoon

Preheat the oven to 350 or 400 degrees F. Meanwhile, place the chicken breasts, one at a time, in a gallon zip lock bag and, using a cast iron skillet, give them a good whack to break the bones and slightly flatten them if not bought already removed. This will help get a more uniform cooking.

Rub the breasts with salt, pepper, smoked paprika and minced garlic. Set aside.

Heat the butter and the oil in a large cast iron pan overmedium-high heat. As soon as the butter turns dark brown, add the chicken breasts skin side down.

Sear for two minutes or until the skin becomes dark golden brown. Flip the breasts and sear for another 2 minutes.

Move the pan into the preheated oven and bake for about 17-20 minutes, until the internal temperature reaches 160F. Remove the breasts from the oven and let them rest for 5 minutes. It's best to remove the breasts from the pan as hot cast iron will continue cooking the meat for too long, this dries out the meat.

MAZE CRAWL

Help baby Alex find his way into his grandmother Mary's arms.

Help Baby Alex find all of the items a baby would need. There are 10 items in total. Write each item you find below...

1. ____________ 2. ____________ 3. ____________
4. ____________ 5. ____________ 6. ____________
7. ____________ 8. ____________ 9. ____________
10. ____________

ALEX AND FRIENDS

Handwritting

Learn to write letters by tracing the alphabet below. Then try your luck at writing the alphabet on the next page.

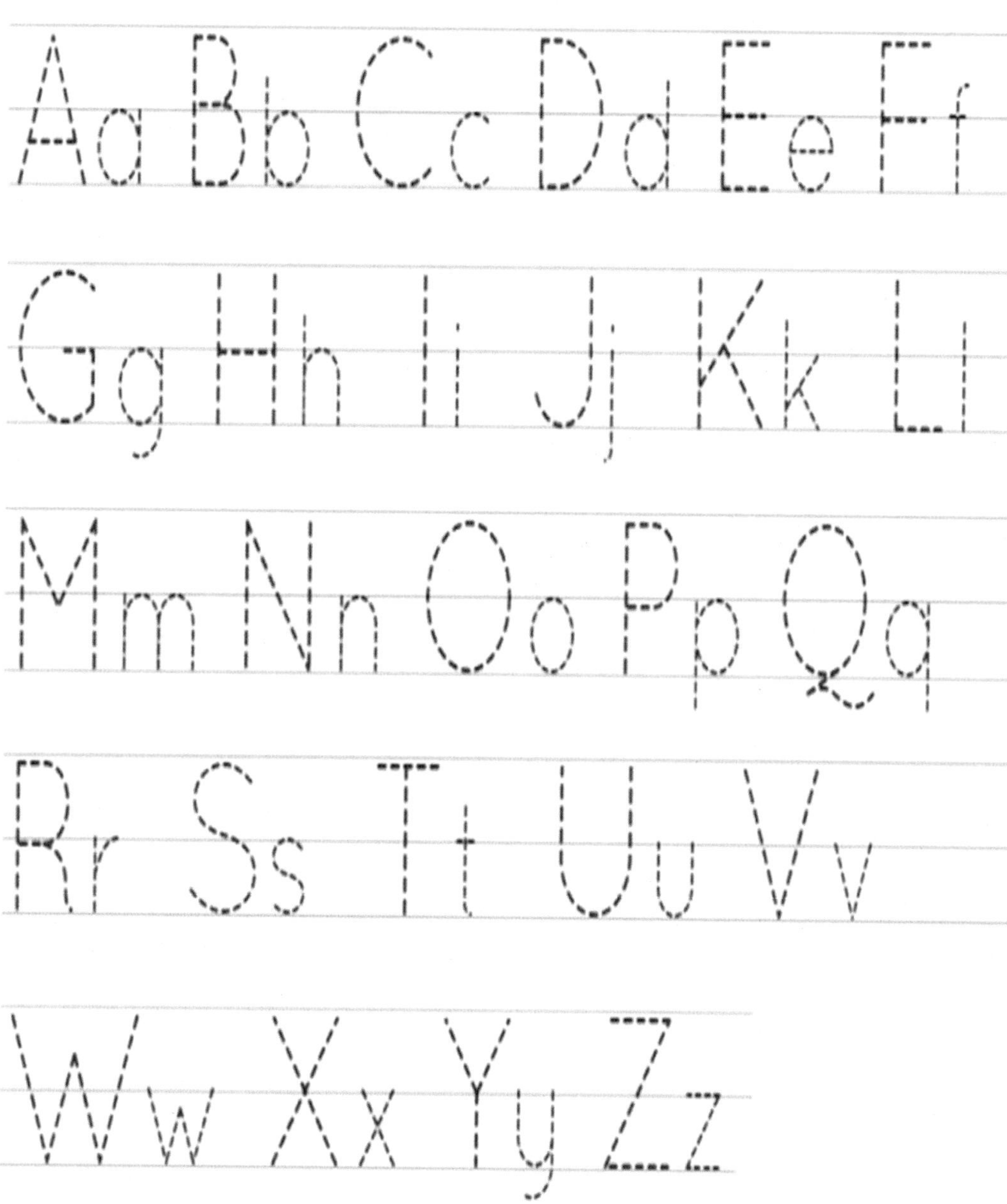

My Best Handwritting

Made in the USA
Columbia, SC
26 April 2021

36671807R00015